Concerning the Book
That Is the Body of the Beloved

Books by Gregory Orr

POETRY

The Caged Owl: New and Selected Poems
(Copper Canyon Press, 2002)

Orpheus & Eurydice
(Copper Canyon Press, 2001)

City of Salt
(University of Pittsburgh Press, 1995)

New and Selected Poems
(Wesleyan University Press, 1988)

We Must Make a Kingdom of It
(Wesleyan University Press, 1986)

The Red House (Harper & Row, 1980)

Gathering the Bones Together (Harper & Row, 1975)

Burning the Empty Nests (Harper & Row, 1973)

CRITICISM

Poetry as Survival (University of Georgia Press, 2002)

Poets Teaching Poets: Self and the World
(edited by Voigt and Orr, University of Michigan Press, 1996)

Richer Entanglements: Essays and Notes on Poetry and Poems
(University of Michigan Press, 1993)

Stanley Kunitz: An Introduction to the Poetry
(Columbia University Press, 1985)

MEMOIR

The Blessing (Council Oak Books, 2002)

CONCERNING THE BOOK
THAT IS THE BODY
OF THE BELOVED

Gregory Orr

Copper Canyon Press

ACKNOWLEDGMENTS

Some of these poems appeared in *Lyric, Meridian, Ninth Letter,*
RATTLE, and *Virginia Quarterly Review.*

Copper Canyon Press is in residence at Fort Worden State Park
in Port Townsend, Washington, under the auspices of Centrum
Foundation. Centrum is a gathering place for artists and
creative thinkers from around the world, students of all ages
and backgrounds, and audiences seeking extraordinary
cultural enrichment.

LIBRARY OF CONGRESS CATALOGING-IN-PUBLICATION DATA

Orr, Gregory.
Concerning the book that is the body
of the beloved / Gregory Orr.
p.   cm.
ISBN 1-55659-229-9 (pbk. : alk. paper)
I. Love poetry, American.   I. Title.
PS3565.R7C66 2005
811'.54 – DC22
2005009892

COPPER CANYON PRESS
Post Office Box 271
Port Townsend, Washington 98368
www.coppercanyonpress.org

For Trisha, Eliza, and Sophia
Beloveds All

CONTENTS

Part One

Part Two

Part Three

Part Four

Part Five

Concerning the Book
That Is the Body of the Beloved

PART ONE

Resurrection of the body of the beloved,
Which is the world.

      Which is the poem
Of the world, the poem of the body.

Mortal ourselves and filled with awe,
We gather the scattered limbs
Of Osiris.

    That he should live again.
That death not be oblivion.

🌱 The beloved is dead. Limbs
And all the body's
Miraculous parts
Scattered across Egypt,
Stained with dark mud.

We must find them, gather
Them together, bring them
Into a single place
As an anthologist might collect
All the poems that matter
Into a single book, a book
Which is the body of the beloved,
Which is the world.

❦ Who wants to lose the world,
For all its tumult and suffering?
Who wants to leave the world,
For all its sorrow?
                              Not I.
And so I come to the Book,
Which is also the body
Of the beloved. And so
I come to the poem.
The poem is the world
Scattered by passion, then
Gathered together again
So that we may have hope.

The shape of the Book
Is the door to the grave,
Is the shape of the stone
Closed over us, so that
We may know terror
Is what we pass through
To reach hope, and courage
Is our necessary companion.

The shape of the Book
Is dark as death, and every page
Is lit with hope, glows
With the light of the vital body.

❦ When I open the Book
  I hear the poets whisper and weep,
  Laugh and lament.

  In a thousand languages
  They say the same thing:
  "We lived. The secret of life
  Is love, which casts its wing
  Over all suffering, which takes
  In its arms the hurt child,
  Which rises green from the fallen seed."

It's not magic; it isn't a trick.
Every breath is a resurrection.
And when we hear the poem
Which is the world, when our eyes
Gaze at the beloved's body,
We're reborn in all the sacred parts
Of our own bodies:
                              the heart
Contracts, the brain
Releases its shower
Of sparks,
                    and the tear
Embarks on its pilgrimage
Down the cheek to meet
The smiling mouth.

❧ Sadness is there, too.
All the sadness in the world.
Because the tide ebbs,
Because wild waves
Punish the shore
And the small lives lived there.
Because the body is scattered.
Because death is real
And sometimes death is not
Even the worst of it.

If sadness did not run
Like a river through the Book,
Why would we go there?
What would we drink?

Isis kneels on the banks
Of the Nile. She is assembling
The limbs of Osiris.
Her live limbs moving
Above his dead, moving
As if in a dance, her torso
Swaying, her long arms
Reaching out in a quiet
Constant motion.

And the river below her
Making its own motions,
Eddies and swirls, a burbling
Sound the current makes
As if a throat was being cleared,
As if the world was about to speak.

❦ The poem is written on the body,
And the body is written on the poem.

The Book is written in the world,
And the world is written in the Book.

This is the reciprocity of love
That outwits death. Death looks
In one place and we're in the other.

Death looks there, but we are here.

❧ "What is life?"
                    When you first
        Hear that question
        It echoes in your skull
        As if someone shouted
        In an empty cave.

        The same answer each time:
        The resurrection of the body
        Of the beloved, which is
        The world.

        Every poem different but
        Telling the same story.
        And we've been gathering
        Them in a book
        Since writing began
        And before that as songs
        Or poems people memorized
        And recited aloud
        When someone asked: "What is life?"

❧ The things that die
Do not die,
Or they die briefly
To be born again
In the Book.

Did you think
You would see
The loved one again
In this world
Or in some other?

No, that cannot happen.
But we have been
Gathering, all of us,
The scattered remnants
Of the loved one
Since the beginning.

In Egypt, the loved
One is not in the pyramids
But in the poem
Carved in stone
About the lover's lips
And eyes.
        In the igloo
The poem gathers
The dark hair of the beloved.

All the poems of the world
Have been gathering the beloved's
Body against your loss.
Read in the Book. Open
Your eyes and your heart;
Open your voice.
                    The beloved
Is there and was never lost.

❦ I read the Book for years
        And never understood a word.
        Scrawled in its margins.
        Wrote my own versions
        Of what I read there,
        But never got a thing right.

        Didn't understand that each
        Poem was a magic spell.
        Was a voice,
        And under that voice: an echo
        That was the spell.

        As if each poem clearly spoke
        The word "Death"
        And the echo said "Life."

        Echo roiling the poem's surface
        As the angel was said
        To trouble the waters
        Of Bethesda's pool in Jerusalem
        So that the first person
        To enter the water
        After the angel had been there
        Was healed.

❧ I've known grief. I don't
Take it lightly. Know how
It gnaws your bones hollow
So you're afraid to stand up,
Afraid the lightest wind will
Knock you over, blow you away.

But maybe the wind is supposed
To blow right through you;
Maybe you're a tree in winter
And your poem translates
That cold wind into song.

❧ I want to go back
    To the beginning.
    We all do.
                I think:
    Hurt won't be there.

    But I'm wrong.
    Where the water
    Bubbles up
    At the spring:
    Isn't that a wound?

How easy to give up hope.
How easy to draw death over you
Like a black cloak. Cover
Your face, your eyes. Stand
There like a dead tree.
I did that, claiming it was penance,
Claiming I was sorry I was
Alive after the beloved died.

Who was I fooling? No one
Demanded I act that way,
Least of all the ones I loved
Who longed to live again
And could not unless I uttered
Their names, unless I told
Their stories, unless I felt
In my own bones
How much they loved the world.

❦ There's nothing occult going on:
   It's not as if the skull opens
   Along its ancient fissures
   Like a bone lotus spreading
   Its petals so as to let a blue
   Light leak out.
                        Nothing
   At all like that. No magic.
   What happens is natural:
   The heart uttering its hurt
   And its happiness: syllables
   Whose rhythm captures
   The pulse of sorrow or joy,
   The slow ache or throb of it.

   And what occurs next can be
   Explained by the physics of feeling,
   By that science through which
   Emotion becomes motion,
   Love jolting the sleeper awake.

❧ Can a river flow beside itself?
Can two bodies move together
Through time?
                    Or are they
Time itself: a liquid motion
Over stasis?
                    Some say Osiris
Was the Nile. And the banks
It overflowed. And the green
Stalks rising though the rich mud.
That the whole cycle of flood
And renewal was love.

❦ When Sappho wrote:
  "Whatever one loves most
  Is beautiful," she began
  The poems of heart's praise
  That comprise the Book
  Of the body of the beloved
  Which is the world.

  Everything in the Book
  Flows from that single poem
  Or the countless others
  That say the same thing
  In other words, other ways.

❦ How radiant and pale
The winter sycamore branches
From which the outer bark
Has peeled and fallen
Like gray rags.
                        What a gift
That the leaves do not
Obscure its nakedness.

The risen body. The risen
Body of the beloved
Still in this world.

❧ Salt on the roads melts
the ice. Salt on the heart
Hardens it.
                    That's not
How the Book
Preserves the body.

The bitten tongue
Tastes blood. The tongue
Uttering, utters love.

❧ The river has a single song,
Which is itself.
The tree has a song.
The bird also.
The heart knows all
These songs
And a million of its own.

Neither the river
Nor the bird can write.
The tree moves
Its branches against
The sky all day
As if it's thinking
About inventing
Its own alphabet,
But nothing comes of it.

So it's still up to us.
We're supposed to bring
Them into the Book,
Make a place for them in our poems.

The world comes into the poem,
The poem comes into the world.
Reciprocity – it all comes down
To that.
                As with lovers:
When it's right you can't say
Who is kissing whom.

Smart or dumb? Who cares?
High or low? It makes no difference.

The head and the heart – which
One's on top? Doesn't matter
As long as both take part.

The poem can't tell the difference.
No, that's not true: It knows,
But still it reads us
With indifference, reads us all the same.

❦ Those who wake in the middle
   Of the night read a different book.
   For one thing, the world's all dark
   around them, as if it disappeared.
   The poems they read are anxious,
   As if they feared the world
   Might not return next morning
   Or if it did might bring them
   Sorrow or bad news. More sorrow,
   More bad news.
                     A little light
   On the book's white pages
   While they read for an hour:
   Pages lit up like a sail at dawn.

   The boat alone on the sea
   But the wind steady, pulling them along.

❦ If death, then grief, right?
Well, yes, but also
Relief, release. And love
That goes past death, that
Keeps the connection
So many think death severs.

And then, of course, there's joy,
Because what we're after
Is the fact of resurrection –
That what the heart longs for
The poem accomplishes:
Praise that lifts up the body
Of the beloved. That wasn't
A grave, only a door that closed
And now is open, opening into a poem.

❧ Suppose you could evoke
The entire body of the beloved
In a single poem.
Would it be all nouns?
All verbs?
            Would it
Contain the word "I"?
Or would that pronoun be
"Understood" as in Chinese
Poems, where it seldom occurs
Since it is known to preside
At the center of all things,
Present by its absence,
Absent as a presence?

Which makes it resemble
The body of the beloved
Called back from oblivion
By all the poems in the Book.

❧ Those dreams in which a phantom
Of the beloved appears: those
Are a true haunting. A trick
Of the mind to make you think
She's lost, that he will never
Come again.
                    You wake
In the dark, weeping. You hear
The river outside your window,
Flowing to the sea. You think:
Who could read poems
In this darkness? And all the time
Your sorrow is the poem of hope
And the beloved is there beside you.

❦ Everything dies. Nothing dies.
That's the story of the Book.

If the Book were a bird
Those two sentences
Would be its wings.

Nothing dies. Everything dies.
If the Book were a fish
They would be its fins.

But the Book is the body
Of the beloved:
Two hands, two feet,
Two eyes.
                    Lips to kiss.

❦ Silence. Does silence
Make things vanish?
Or confirm
their disappearance?
Is the beloved
Who has died
Buried more deeply
By silence
Than by earth?

Even closed
And locked away
The Book whispers
About the beloved
In dreams. Still,
It's a whispering
Difficult to understand,
Impossible almost.

But if we find
The Book and open it,
If we find the poem
That is trying to find us,
The poem the beloved
Wrote and sent out
On the long journey
Toward our heart – if
We find that poem,

It all makes sense
And the silence recedes
Before the beloved's
Quiet voice speaking to us.

❧ The beloved has gone away.
   Always, this is the case.
   Each moment turns on its hinge
   And loss is there, loss
   Announcing itself as an absence.

   But that's because we're looking
   Backward, looking in the wrong
   Direction: so desperately clinging
   To a last glimpse of the beloved,
   As if loss itself is what we loved.

   And all the time the beloved
   Is coming toward us, is arriving
   Out of the future, eager to greet us.

♧ Some of the poems are clear.
Some are incomprehensible.
Aspects of the beloved:
Sometimes she's plain
As a pebble; others,
He's hidden in opacity
Like a tree's roots.

It's not all lucid miracle.
You knew that. Life itself
Was full of mystery –
Why shouldn't the life
After death be strange?

Tears and laughter –
Weighing them out,
One against the other.
Sobs and love-sighs:
Trying to separate them,
Putting each in the scales.

What a job! The Book's
No help. Clarification,
Catharsis, coherence:
Every poem in the Book
Aspires to these ideals,
But to no avail.

It's all there, but
Hopelessly jumbled
And muddled.
Tossed in the same sack.
You want to sort it out
And come to some conclusion
And instead
You're tossed in, too.

❦ Reading and writing poems
For more than forty years,
And all the time believing
They helped me live.
I was right. But I was also
Wrong, or at least I missed a lot.

Loss seemed to me the most of it.
I believed in love but I thought
Its name was loss.
                              And worse:
When I said "life" I meant "death."
When I said "death"
I have no idea what I meant.

But the body is real, and the world
Also. And the beloved's body
Is a palpable, beautiful thing.

And poems are real: the body
Writes them, thinking bodies,
Thinking the world.

❧ Lighten up, lighten up.
Let go of the heaviness.
Was it a poem from the Book
That so weighed you down?

Impossible. Less than a feather.
Less than the seed a milkweed
Pod releases in the breeze.

Lifted, it drifts out to settle
In a field, with all that's inside it
Waiting to become
Root and tendril, to come alive.

✤ Too many mysteries. Too many
  Emotions. Why don't we stop
  Adding to the Book?
  Why don't we let it rest
  In neglect for a few generations?

  Could we? Is it in our power?
  I've sat by it and seen it expand
  Without anyone opening
  Its covers to add a page.
  I've seen it grow as if someone
  Had merely thought a poem.

PART TWO

To feel, to feel, to feel.
Failing that, why live?
Might as well be a coffin
Drifting on a gray flood.

"The feel of not to feel"—
That counts, too.
Anguish is one clear
Sign we're still here.

But we all need help.
The beloved's there,
And the world also.
And then there's the Book.

Poem after poem, song
Upon song. And all
With the same chorus:
"Wake up, you're alive."

Sometimes happy, sometimes sad.
Or the old parable my wife
Likes to tell: "Good luck,
Bad luck? Who knows?"
We're deep in the mystery of it
And it's deep in us.

Loss behind. The unknown
Ahead. Lifting up
The light of the poem
Like a lantern. Stepping out
Bravely into the dark.

❧ Or is it loss ahead as well as
Loss behind? You could think
That way, could easily believe that.
If so, better pay attention to the moment:
It's all you've got.
                              That
And the Book. The Book
Which is outside time and inside it
Also. Which has gathered every poem.
Every particle of the beloved.
The body's whole and complete,
Palpable and alive. Just like this moment.

✤ Concentrating on those motions
That show hope most simply:
The hoe clearing the irrigation
Ditch so the water flows.
The green stalks poking up
Through the dark, Nilotic mud:
So many tongues uttering
Their joy.
              Or is it *our* joy
They utter? Who saw Osiris
Buried, his corpse swollen
And deformed by death.
Who wept above the spot
Where he lay a long time
In the earth, listening
To the whisper of worms.
And now it is spring
And the beloved returns:
Who was fat with death
Is slender as a sapling now.
And silent grief gives way –
we shout our joy as fields
shout their green shoots.

In our despair we were dead
As the earth in winter, dark
And inert. Now the world
Is reborn. Now the poem
Of the dead one
Comes alive in our hearts.

❧ To lose the loved one –
Is anything worse?
To die one's self –
Not desirable,
But far easier
Than living on past
The loss of the beloved.

So much of your heart
There in the grave.
And what comes in
To fill the emptiness?
Shame at being alive.
As if to survive means
You betrayed the beloved.

Then life is a penance
And tastes bitter.
You look at the dirt
At your feet; you
Never gaze at a face
Or lift your eyes
Toward the night sky.

You eat and talk and sleep
But you're really dead.
And all the time, the beloved
Is alive in the Book,
Waiting for you,
Eager to speak to you,

Eager to hear all the secrets
You've stored up in your grief
As if your body was a grave.

Eager to hear your voice.
Curious to know why
You withheld yourself,
Why you buried your love.

❧ Even the saddest poems have journeyed
Past death and been resurrected
As words on a page. Death never
Stopped the simplest poem. Death
Starts them, loss launches them out
Into the future, so they will someday
Wash ashore on the beautiful
Page of the Book: message scratched
On a log or lodged in a bottle:
"I write to you from the world."

❦ Nothing more beautiful than the body
Of the beloved that is the world.

Nothing more beautiful than the voice
Of the beloved, calling our name.

In so many poems, we hear it.
In so many poems, we answer.

✿ Someone else called out
   To the beloved
   And we were jealous.
   She turned her head,
   As if she heard a voice;
   His face went suddenly
   Vague and faraway.

   Then anger came over us.
   We ourselves could have
   Destroyed the beloved;
   Could have wrecked
   The world in our rage.

   Had the lesson ended there
   We would have been humbled
   And left alone in the void
   Of death.
                 But everything
   Passes. The passion swept
   Over us like a huge wave:
   We were lifted and tossed down.
   But we did not drown.

❦ Why should the grave be final?
Why should death be everything?
Isn't the world wonderful?
Don't we want more of it?
And in poems, life goes on
Forever.
             Life and more life
Piled up in the Book.
Intensities and griefs
And pleasures accumulating
From centuries past, for centuries
To come.
And laughing at the notion
Of centuries, laughing
Not at time
But at the idea of finality.

for Floyd Skloot

✤ Listening to Bach's solo suites
   For cello, you know
   He's found the poem
   But not the words,
   Doesn't need the words.

   And the words don't matter
   When the mother weeps
   Over her dead child.

   Some of the most important
   Poems don't get written down,
   But you'll find them in the Book.

❦ Now the snow is falling
Even more than an hour ago.
The pine in the backyard
Bows with the weight of it.

Two years ago, my father
Died. What love we had,
Hidden under misery,
Weighed down with years
Of silence.

And now,
Maybe the poem can release
Us, maybe the poem can express
The love and let the rest
Slide to the earth as the snow
Does now, freeing the tree
Of its burden.

❦ It's winter and I think of spring.
It's dark and I feel the light
That comes out of the body
Of the beloved, that fills
The room as it filled the life.

Alone in the dark you are
A body, and the Book
Is another body, is the body
Of the other: the beloved
Which is the world.

Time isn't a door that only
Opens to shut; time isn't
The lamp that's on,
Then clicks off.
Time is the great wheel of it,
Winter then spring, time
Is the great whirl of it:
The dance in which we hold
Close the body of the beloved,
Hold tight for dear life.

❧ I never planned to die.
I never expected to be reborn.
I didn't give much thought
To anything, until
The Book let me know
The score. The Book
Did most of the talking.

"Where is your mother?"
The Book asked, as if
I was a lost child.

"She's gone," I answered.

"How is it then, I saw her
Inside me and talked with her,
As I talked with all the mothers,
Listened to all the fathers
Who spoke of their sons
And their daughters
And the lonely ones who had
No sons or daughters?"

All that between two covers?
In a book the size of a matchbox?
You have to open it.
If you want to see the light,
You have to strike the match.

❦ When my kids look for me I hope
They can find me in the house
Or reach me by phone.

When that won't work,
I hope they find me in the Book,
In a poem or song someone wrote,
Or in one of my own.
                              That anthology
That is the body of the beloved,
Which is the world.

❧ How small the eyes of hate.
I'm not making this up
Or being metaphorical.
A man held a gun against
My head and I saw how
Small his eyes were
With what they refused
To take in of the world.
This happened beside
A small highway
In Alabama in 1965.
What history called
The Civil Rights
Movement; what I call
The tiny eyes of hate.

❧ How large the eyes of love.
How the pupils dilate
With desire (I'm not
Making this up: science
Has proved it's true).

Those eyes wide
And glistening: gates
Thrown open. What's
Inside, free to flow
Out as feeling,
And the whole world
And the beloved
Welcome to enter.

❦ Scratched with a stick in snow
　　Or with fingernails into a prison wall.
　　Or drawn with spittle
　　Stained with blood.
　　　　　　　　　　　　Or composed
　　Whole in the mind and not written
　　Down until the poet was safe,
　　Until the danger had passed.

　　But the danger doesn't pass:
　　The risk is always there.
　　And the challenge, too:
　　To take it in, to feel it, and then
　　To speak it back in poems and songs,
　　Or in the silence that burns under
　　The numb surface as a river moves
　　Under its armor of ice.
　　　　　　　　　　　　To be alive
　　Is one thing. To die is another.
　　To be reborn in poems in the Book
　　Is a third and final thing
　　that has no end.

❧ To become the tree,
  That's easy.
  To *be* the flower,
  Not so hard.
  But to become the beloved,
  That's not allowed.
  The distance between you:
  Crucial as the poem
  That bridges it.
  That space between your two
  Bodies, no matter how closely
  Pressed: it's essential,
  It defines what it is to be
  In the world: surrounded
  By infinite space, balanced
  On the point of a pin,
  Spinning there,
  Singing your song.

❦ Could it all be said in a single poem
And not be completely cryptic?
There's Issa's haiku about
His daughter's death:

"This world of dew
Is only a world of dew.
And yet, ah, and yet...."

How the two lines seem to accept
That life is ephemeral,
And then that last:
A cry of quiet anguish.

Accept, but protest. Yield,
Then resist.
                    The heart
Would have it both ways.
To see the world and say it true
Means starting with loss.
But that's not what the heart wants,
That's not where the saying stops.

for Sam Hamill

❦ Who can measure the gratitude
   Of the beloved?
   To have lain so long in the dark,
   Listening to the worms whisper.
   The eyes closed, the nerves numb.
   And then to be brought alive.

   And all because of you.
   Because you sang the song
   That someone wrote – or
   Hummed it, even, not remembering
   The words, but feeling the feeling of it.

❧ When we're young there's lots
We don't know about
The beloved:
How he or she is only housed
Briefly in this or that body.
Mostly, the beloved is the world,
But we're not ready to see
That yet, not able to bear
The idea that the beloved
Won't necessarily gaze back at us
With eyes like ours, won't
Wrap us in his or her arms.

We want risk, but comfort, too,
Comfort most of all.
We're still clinging to our loneliness,
Not yet ready to be alone.

❦ To add our own suffering
   To the world's: tempting
   When we're young,
   Easy to confuse that
   With love.
                   As if
   The beloved desired
   Our sacrifice, wanted
   Us to be the moth
   Impaling itself
   On the candle's radiant
   Thorn.
                We'd only
   Smother the flame.
   What the beloved wants
   Is to burn more brightly,
   To have more life.

To hold a pane of glass
Up to the world, to a part
Of the world: to see clearly
What's there and see it framed
In the shape of a page.

Can a poem do that? Be
bald and alert as a photograph?
Who knows? The self is not
A clear lens. Emotions distort;
What we see appears closer
Or further away, or warped.

And that's the truth of poems:
Both the wanting to lucidly see
And the warp of our passions,
And a third thing:
Discovering ourselves
Lightly reflected
in the glass we look through.

❧   Nesting dolls. Inside the body
    Of the beloved, the body
    Of the Book; inside that:
    The body of the world.

    Next time you look
    It's all reversed.

❦ Of course, a book about living
  Has to be filled with dying.
  And a book of joy
  Will be full of sorrow.
  Why else winter?
  Why else the bones
  Of trees against the gray sky?

  But could you stay in winter?
  Could you brace your shoulder
  Against the great wheel
  And halt its slow roll?
  Could you stop a single bush
  From sending out its new
  leaves, from flowering?

❧ When you are sad
The Book grows larger
As if to comfort you.

When you despair
It can narrow
To a single poem.

And when joy
Arrives – hard
To read at all.
Blinking at
Page-dazzle;
The words
Breaking apart
Into letters,
Dancing there,
Unable to calm down.

❧ To be alive: not just the carcass
But the spark.
That's crudely put, but...

If we're not supposed to dance,
Why all this music?

❦ Calm down, calm down.
But why calm down?
When I'm dead and only
A poem in the Book
Read by someone
Not yet born,
Then I'll be calm.
Then I'll tell them
In a quiet voice
What a miracle it is
To be alive. I won't
Shout and jump around.
I'll whisper it in her ear.

And if I'm lucky
She'll shout and jump
Around; her heart
Will beat a little faster.

❦ So obvious that the voice can cease
But the song doesn't stop.
That's why we have these marks
On the page. If it was only
The palpable body before us,
If it was only the voice speaking,
It would be brief, would stop
When the breath stopped,
Would be a small, ephemeral thing.

But it isn't small. It's huge.
It has all of history in its shortest
Song. Empires rise and fall
In a couplet; fortresses tumble
Down and become owl-haunted
In a haiku's handful of syllables.

And empires aren't what matters,
Nor the ambitions of violent men.
Not according to this Book.
Not according to the beloved.

❧ Facing away from the light,
I looked at the world,
But so much of it
Was obscured
By my own long shadow.

Turned around now, I see
Each object
Gilded and glowing
In the sun, know
The sum of them
Is the beautiful
Body of the beloved,
Which is the world.

❦ Weeping, weeping, weeping.
No wonder the oceans are full;
No wonder the seas are rising.

It's not the beloved's fault.
Dying is part of the story.
It's not your fault either:
Tears are also.
                    But
You can't read when you're
Crying. Sobbing, you won't
Hear the song that resurrects
The body of the beloved.

Why not rest a while? If weeping
Is one of the world's tasks,
It doesn't lack adherents.
Someone will take your place,
Someone will weep for you.

❧ The human heart
   Is a labyrinth.
   One more reason
   To explore it.

   It's dark and confusing
   Inside us.
   Doesn't the poem bring light?

❧ To loll in a sensual torpor –
That's fun for the young.

If we had not lost the beloved
We, too, would be lulled
By the body's pleasures,
We, too, would have despised
The songs of grief,
Which are the deepest
Songs of love, those
Low moans, close cousins
Of the quiet cries of lust
As it's gratified.

❧ I saw my own body
    Stiff and dead
    Under a tree.
    I saw the beloved
    Bend over my corpse
    And breathe life
    In through my mouth.

    And again I was alive
    Inside. I felt my lips
    Loosen and shape
    The vowels of desire.
    I knew I would rise
    And walk in the fields.
    I felt love move
    Through my veins,
    Felt it move through
    All things in the world.

❦ How to exhaust the inexhaustible?
    The world can't stop giving.
    Nor can the beloved.

    When the beloved dies
    It's only to ask more of you,
    So you become richer from giving.

❧ Time to shut up.
Voltaire said the secret
Of being boring
Is to say everything.

And yet I held
Back about love
All those years:
Talking about death
Insistently, even
As I was alive;
Talking about loss
As if all was loss,
As if the world
Did not return
Each morning.
As if the beloved
Didn't long for us.

No wonder I go on
So. I go on so
Because of the wonder.

❧ We'd only just met, were
Driving in your car
When the axle broke
In a small town. No hotel,
No money. We had
To sleep in a field.
It was dark when we lay
Down. Cold, though
It was summer. Trying
To stay warm with all
Our clothes on. For a while
I was the blanket and you
The body, then the other
Way around: one on top
And then the other. And
In the middle of the night
We argued because you took
Your boots off. I thought
You would be more cold;
You knew the boots were too
Tight, the circulation
Cut off, better bare feet
Than that. And a skunk
Wandered by in the dark,
So close we could hear it
As well as smell it.
And at dawn we found
We'd slept by a pond,
And a kingfisher paused
On a branch above it.

Its iridescent feathers.
And on a hill across
The small valley, the name
Of the town spelled out
In white rocks: Castle
Creek. This story is true
And happened thirty years
Ago. And did we know then
We'd be together still?
Which is the beloved,
Which is the world.

for Trisha

❧ Snow on the tree branch.
Vanished by noon.

That feeling I had,
It's gone, too.

Something about
The wonder of it.

Poem of the snow
On the tree branch.

It's still there.

❧ Tired of the body?
Tired of the poem
Of the body?

               Rest awhile.
Even the most passionate
Lovers paused. Even
The fiercest warriors
Put down their swords,
Exhausted by slaughter.

❦ You might think the things I say
   Are too simple for words,
   Too embarrassing to be spoken.

   But if I repeat the obvious,
   Where's the harm in that?

   Maybe it was always simple:
   Loss surrounds us.
   Who would deny it?

   We ourselves are loss, are lost.
   But those who came before us
   Left the Book as a guide,
   The Book full of songs and poems.

PART THREE

❧ All the different books you read –
You were searching
For the one Book.

All the poems you read
And what you really sought
Was the one poem.

And when you found it
Weren't you lifted up?
Didn't you become lighter?

Transparent even, so that
someone looking at you
Could see the world,
Could see the world inside you?

❧ You can read the world
Without words:
Eyes take in its dazzle.

And you can read the body
Of the beloved by touch.

You can do that much,
And all of it's magic, but
Neither body nor world
Can be born again
Except by tongue.

And to live once only –
What if that's not enough?

❧ How badly the world needs words.
Don't be fooled
By how green it is,
How it seems to be thriving.

"Willow" rescues that tree
From its radiant perishing.

How much more so then
When you name the beloved.

✿ How the crocus pops up:
  Leafless stalk and purple
  Blossom-cup out of bare mud!

  As if it couldn't wait any longer.
  Not even the grass has ventured forth.
  Ice and snow could still return.

  What does the beloved care?
  So eager to begin again,
  To welcome the new life.

🌱 The dandelion, too.
First, it's a plush sun,
Then, before you know it,
It's become a ghostly globe –
And of its two forms,
Who can say
Which is more lovely?

As if you had to choose
Between the glorious world
And the words that resurrect it.

❧ Oh, I know: the beloved
Every time. Always the beloved.

But the beloved is gone.

We could lie down on the ground
And weep our lives away.
We could stamp our feet and refuse
Like little children.

And what would that accomplish?

Better to sing our sorrow song.

It's only words. But it's words
That bring the beloved back.

❀ They said to me: here
Is the beloved
And here is the world:
You have to choose.

Here is the heart
And all it can hold;
Here is the having
And all you can grasp.

False. Stop right there.
How do we know
We can't have both?

Would that be greed,
When the two are one?

❦ Let's remake the world with words.
Not frivolously, nor
To hide from what we fear,
But with a purpose.
                        Let's,
As Wordsworth said, remove
"The dust of custom" so things
Shine again, each object arrayed
In its robe of original light.

And then we'll see the world
As if for the first time,
As once we gazed at the beloved
Who was gazing at us.

In the spring swamp
The red-winged blackbird
Perched on a cattail stalk:
Have you heard its song?
If you have, no need of heaven.
No need of divine resurrection.

It's one of those birdsongs
That hold a spot in the Book,
Saving that space until
A human song comes along
Worthy to replace
All that wordless love.

❦ Weighed down with the weight
Of the world. What can lift you?
And how did it become so heavy?
Is it because the beloved left?

How dark those rocks seem now.
That tree shadow more solid
Than the tree itself.
                    Help,
Help is on the way. The beloved
Is coming. A cloud over the sun
Doesn't mean there is no sun.

❧ Humid morning.
  Last night's rain becomes
  Sun-dapple on lawns.

  Earthworm on the walk,
  Doing its slow dance
  In honor of the world.

❧ The sun: a hot hand
On your body;
The shade, a cool one.

Summer. The beloved
Presses close.

❦ No one is grateful
For such a loss.
But could ingratitude
Stave it off?
Could bitterness
Hold it at bay?

On the other side
Your job begins –
Where the beloved's
Body lies.
              Only
Your words can revive
Her, only your love
Can make him live again.

How could that Chinese poet,
Dead three thousand years,
Know how much
We love the world?

If only we could talk
To him as he talks
To us in his poem.
If only we could say
How much his words
Mean to us.
                    Quick,
Write it down in the Book.
Send it to him.
Three thousand years from now.

❦ July sun on the green leaves
   Of that chestnut tree,
   Intense as when ancient armies
   Beat their swords on their shields.

   The beloved marches toward us,
   Cannot be resisted.
   Throw down our weapons
   And beg for mercy.
   This much love defeats us.

Hummingbird's furious
Hot heart
Beating without surcease.
How can those tiny wings
Cool it?
        The poem
Of the beloved –
Such intensity
It can hardly breathe.

❧ Whitman's list of the things he could see
As he sat, half paralyzed,
An old man by a woodland pond.

The names of the different trees.
The birds he glimpsed or only heard
Yet recognized by their songs.

The bushes and grasses that grew there.

How happy those lists made him:
Tamarack, birch, maple, larch....

Gazing from where he loafed
On the bank, or from the pond itself
Where he floated naked
In the round pool of it:

As if he were the pupil
In a wide-open eye.

And the trees around it
Delicate and strong as lashes.

Oh, the world, the world,
What eye is wide enough?
What pupil sufficiently diligent?

Let's put our poems in the Book,
Let's add what we see to the beautiful list.

for Jake Berthot

❦ Today only a single poem.
  This one.
  So small.

  In the Middle Ages
  Angels frolicked
  On the head of a pin –
  Spacious as a ballroom.

  Have faith.
  The beloved approaches,
  Robed in radiance,
  Dressed in language,
  Eager to dance.

❧ Waking now, and we didn't even know
We'd been asleep in our luckiness.
A luckiness that now has ceased;
That the beloved's death
Has ended.
                    Seeing the world
Differently, seeing it clearly
Or through a fog of grief,
But seeing it, where before
There had been no world,
Only the beloved blocking the light,
Only the beloved filling our sight.

❧ No one I ever believed said:
  "There is no death."

  Besides, I don't want to live
  Forever. Already, I'm forgetting
  Things, not just names and dates
  But also moments and places
  I cherished.
                And I'm feeling
  Old: certain parts
  Of my body always ache.

  "To love forever." Now that's
  A different matter. That's
  What the Book teaches me,
  That's why I keep reading.

❦ The beloved often
Arrives in disguise.
Not to avoid you,
Not to elude you
Who long so.
That would be cruel.

No. Only to surprise you.
To find you before
You find her.
To recognize you
Before you recognize him.

❧ Spasm and sadness.
A little kiss, then
A little chasm.

It could give passion
A bad name.

Luckily, the Book
Has a thing or two
To say about this.

❧ To Guillaume Apollinaire, the beloved
Was *"La Jolie Rousse"* – "the beautiful
redhead."

    He fought in World War I
And was seriously wounded.
But his beloved's red hair
Was not the color of war or blood.
It was the radiant color of love.

To him, the beloved was adventure:
Her red hair a flag in the distance,
Rallying him, commanding him
To venture forward into the unknown.

He followed her.
He left behind his books, his poem.

❦ Saying the word
Is seizing the world.

Not by the scruff,
Not roughly,
But still fervent,
Still the fierce hug of love.

❧ Not the first lessons of grief—
They are all about sorrow.
But stay to the end of the teaching,
Where grief reads from the Book,
Reads a poem you never heard before,
A poem about the beloved.

It talks about how he thinks
Constantly of us, and
How we miss her so.

And how we meet in the poem.

❧ We exist in the mortal world only,
But the beloved persists
Beyond also. He or she
Starts here, starts as a body
Of flesh and blood (and oh,
It's so lovely),
But that's not enough.
How could that be enough?

And so our longing calls out
Past those limits, calls out
Into the void.
                    And the beloved
Answers from all directions,
Answers from every page in the Book.

❦ Skitterbugs on the stream's surface.
Poems in the Book.

Zipping here, then there;
Nervous, elusive, shooting off
At absurd angles.
                            Harmless
Creatures. Can't be caught
In the quickest hand.

Silly-looking.
But the water they move on
Is clear and deep.

for Sophie

❧ How is it I'm tired,
And the beloved is lively?

Easy answer: the beloved
Is always ready for love.

Can't we rest awhile,
Can't we sleep?
                    You sleep,
The beloved replies,
I'll stay up and watch the stars.
I'll become the world.

❦ The grapes taste good.
I hope whoever grew
Them and picked them
Was paid well.

The poems in the Book:
Free as the air
They're made of.

What a business:
Praising the beloved.
What a business:
Loving the world.

❧ Some say you're lucky
If nothing shatters it.

But then you wouldn't
Understand poems or songs,
You'd never know
Beauty comes from loss.

It's deep inside every person:
A tear tinier
Than a pearl or thorn.

It's one of the places
Where the beloved is born.

for Liza

❧ When you're afraid,
You're afraid
Of something.

When you dread,
It's Nothing
That you dread
(so the philosopher
said).
      Nothing
Can be
Terrifying.
But don't get
Confused: a blank
Page in the Book
Isn't Nothing.

It's something
Waiting to happen,
It's the beloved
Holding her breath,
Hoping you'll write or call.

❦ How can lines
Zigzag down
Like lightning?

How did Emily
Dickinson
Write those poems?

The beloved must
Have stood
Beside her,
Handing her words
Like spears.

What a nightstorm
In the heart.
Each word
Bursting
Its ghastly flash
Followed by sudden dark.

🌱 The poet approaches the lectern –
We've bought another lottery
Ticket, made another investment
In the effort to express human
Passion in a shareable way.

If the poems are bad, the hour
Will seem to go on forever.
If a single poem moves us,
Or even a single line,
We'll enter eternity briefly
And the gift will shine.

PART FOUR

❧ Bittersweet, bittersweet –
Sappho's word. She made it
Up – the complex taste
Of love.

       First, your whole
Mouth shudders and chokes,
Your tongue revolts.

              Then,
The sweetness bursts
And floods.

        Fruit of love,
Bitter, then sweet;
Loss, then restoration.
We eat and we eat.

❧ Ripeness of summer,
Yet autumn is here.

Fruit fat on the trees,
But already the leaves
Brown and curl at their edges.

Fruit and seed in the heart
Of the fruit – apple or pear.
Already something
Preparing to rot and die,
And something inside
Ready to live again.

❧ Wildness of the world,
Branches tossing in a storm.
Yet the beloved seemed so mild,
Seemed calm at the center
Even when passion swept her,
Even when he lost control.

Quiet surface of the world
And wildness at the center:
The beloved gazes in a mirror
That turns everything inside out.

And the Book. Sometimes
It's a rock. Sometimes
Its wings frantically beat
Inside an invisible cage.

There's the daisy: white petals
And a plush yellow center.
And so we begin
Our anxious interrogation:
"She loves me,
She loves me not."
Plucking it bare
Like a plump chicken
We plan to cook.

Daisy comes from
"Day's eye" – the sun.
A flower as metaphor
For the world's splendor.

The beloved shining on us
All the time,
And us with our silly questions.

✤ Yes, our human time is finite:
   That much is obvious.
   But I can hear
   The infinite knocking
   At the door
   Of almost every word.

   And when they open,
   Each of them opens
   Into a world.

🌱 Last night, a huge storm.
Branches torn from the maple,
Plants overturned on the porch,
Spilled from their safe little world,
Their clay pot with its gallon of dirt.

And won't there be worse?
Won't it happen to the people
We love? Then we'll know sorrow.

The branch can't be put back
On the tree. We scoop up
The earth and cover the roots –
Who knows if it will live?

❧ All that sorrow.
    You filled the sink
    With your tears.
    Filled the tub, even.
    And it seemed then
    You could change
    The ocean,
    Could add to it.

    Pull the plug.
    No more blubbering.
    Tears don't bring
    The beloved back.
    Try words.
    Maybe they'll work.

    Since time began,
    Two schools of thought:
    Weeping and words,
    Sorrow and song.

    Words begin in weeping,
    But they're transfigured
    Somehow. They have
    Grief still inside them,
    But outside they shine.

❧ When we lost the beloved,
We lost the world.

A crack opened between
Us and all else.

Briefly, perhaps,
But how deep it was.
Who could forget
What was glimpsed there?

We stepped carefully across
Or leapt and hoped
We'd reach the other side.

But the chasm was real
And we were wordless,
Worldless,
And bereft of love.

Rain last night.
Leaves in the street.
I look up.
      The tree
Is full; not a sign
That a single
Leaf is missing.

Poem in the Book
That seems a lie,
That offends
Your suffering:
Tear it out,
Throw it away.
No harm done.

Tear them all out—
Grief can be that deep.
They'll return
When the time's right.
They'll bring the beloved.

❦ Naked before the beloved.
And the beloved naked
Before us.
            No wonder
The censors get excited.
No wonder the Book
Is seldom mentioned,
Not readily available,
Difficult and risky to find.

No wonder we search for it
All our days. No wonder
We seek just a glimpse of it
And, catching that glimpse,
Are changed.

❦ No postmortems, please.
The world is immortal.
The world renews itself.

What about poems and songs –
Do they perish?
Maybe they only
Vanish awhile,
Maybe they go underground
To gather some other
Knowledge and come back
In another form:

New words, a new melody,
Yet somehow
The same beloved,
Singing the same song.

✿ Oh, to be deeply naked
And still see love
In the beloved's eyes.
To be free of shame.

Was there anything
More wonderful?

How long did it last?
Maybe only a moment;
Maybe it was a dream.
We were afraid
To feel such joy.

Still, it changed us,
And for once we knew
We belonged in the world.

I thought I was hunting
For a poem. Hours spent
Leafing through dusty
Books, huge anthologies.

And all the time, the poem
Was stalking me.
Tiger, burning in the forests
Of the night, eager
To devour my heart.

No, not my whole heart,
Only the rotten parts,
Only what needed
To be renewed.

Only what needed.

❧ Long night on the road.
Huge distance between
Two cities. Distance also
Between radio stations.
Only static coming through.

Stop for coffee at this diner.
Need to wake up. Need
To consult the little book
Of the jukebox and hear
The beloved sing my song.

✿ If we could have the world
   Without the beloved
   Would that suffice?

   Lacks one, lacks both.
   Did you think that heap
   Of objects was the world?

   It only becomes the world
   Because of the beloved:

   She lends it her light;
   His kiss makes it live.

✿ Autumn with its too-muchness,
Stretching the boundaries
Of song.
            The grape
Ripe against its skin –
One more day of sun
And it will burst with joy.

One more day under the beloved's
Gaze, the beloved's sway,
And we will die of love.

❧ Is the beloved greedy,
Demanding all our love?

Is the ocean thirsty,
Drinking all the rivers
And lakes, draining them
Only to fill them full again?

❧ Eyes blurred with tears,
A downcast gaze.
How will we recognize him?
How will we know her face?

Does it occur to you
The beloved is trying to return
And all our grief keeps her away,
Keeps him far from us?

The beloved never intended this.
Left clear instructions
Not to mourn too long
Or too deeply. Left them
In a memorable form:
In a poem in the Book,
In a song.

❧ My mother's joy
Never lasted long.
Her sorrow either.

She walked her path
Into oblivion
Long before I wrote
My first poem.

I see her now,
Resurrected
In my thoughts:

One more beloved
Lighting my way
Into the dark,

One more beloved
Bringing back
From the abyss
Explicable gifts.

❧ What suffering! Why isn't
   The earth covered with tears
   To the very mountain peaks?

   Ah, but it is and always has been.
   And the globe is filled
   To bursting with groans.

   And above it all the Book
   floats like an ark.

   Not serene, but separate
   From all the agony.
   Not indifferent, but other,
   Like the beloved.

   If you can glimpse it
   Among the waves,
   Swim toward it.

❧ What did someone cynically
Say once: open a vein
And let it flow onto the page?

If only one could
And have words result.

Not seeking self-display,
Seeking release.

Seeking the other
Who is lost inside you.

Seeking to say it out;
Your grief and longing
Bringing the resurrection about.

❦ A song of resurrection played
On a leg-bone flute?
I don't think so.

We want more than to just
Make the dust dance;
We want the beloved's
Living presence
Returned to us as song.

Hair, lips, brows, the beautiful
Flesh and features: words
Can evoke them, poems
Can bring them again
To the mind's eye.

Hollow bone into which
We breathe our sorrow.
No, that won't do.
                         Something
So empty, but it's not emptiness
We feel. I think we must
Ourselves become
Both instrument and song,
Full as we are with longing.

❀ The world looks
In all directions
Like that vase
Of chrysanthemums
On the table.
But the beloved
Looks only at you.

How easy to choose.

Yes, the flowers
Are beautiful,

But the beloved's gaze
Makes you beautiful, too.

When the world
For a single moment
Focuses on you,
You become the beloved.

Glowing. Almost unable
To contain your glee.

Precarious bliss,
It was for this, for this....

✾ Not deepest grief,
  Of course,
  Nothing can help you
  With that.
              Later,
  Maybe, but not now.
  Now you are unreachable,
  Alone with all that was
  Awry between you.

  Alone with what was said
  And not said.
                  Saying it all
  Now, freely confessing
  What you withheld then,
  Admitting what you denied
  Only a short while ago.

  How obvious that you
  Were often wrong and unkind.

  Aware now of all the good
  Deeds you intended
  That remained undone.
  Aware of all the good
  Between you
  That death has undone.

If deepest grief is hell,
When the animal self
Wants to lie down
In the dark and die also…

If deepest grief is hell,
Then the world returning
(Not soon, not easily)
Must be heaven.

The joke you laughed at
Must be heaven.
Or the funny thing
The cat did
At its food dish.

Whatever
Guides you back
To the world.

That dark so deep
The tiniest light
Will do.

❧ And it happens, of course:
Harm comes to the beloved.

We must be brave
Even if we don't feel it.
She needs us. He has
No other ally.
Act now. Later for questions
And uncertainty;
Later for fear and second-guessing.

To risk all for the beloved –
How else will we be saved?

❦ This room crowded
   With memories, even this
   Must be emptied.

   Let it go. Let it all
   Go. We must make
   Space for the beloved's
   Return.
            Nothing here
   Is precious, nothing
   We can't live without.

   Or if there is, let it go
   And the beloved
   Will bring it again
   When she returns.

   Let it go, now.
   Even this must be emptied.

❦ Clearing out the room
That had been a shrine
To the beloved.

Now it all seems junk.
Now we must empty
That space, perhaps
Even paint the walls
A new, bright color.

Be brave. Admit it:
All this dusty stuff
Needs to be tossed
In a box and hauled
To a dump.
It's morbid.
It shows a lack of faith.

The beloved was never
These inert objects.
The beloved was alive.

As she is now inside you,
As he is now in the Book.

❧ I put the beloved
   In a wooden coffin.
   The fire ate his body;
   The flames devoured her.

   I put the beloved
   In a poem or song.
   Tucked it between
   Two pages of the Book.

   How bright the flames.
   All of me burning,
   All of me on fire
   And still whole.

☙ Not the loss alone,
   But what comes after.
   If it ended completely
   At loss, the rest
   Wouldn't matter.

   But you go on.
   And the world also.

   And words, words
   In a poem or song:
   Aren't they a stream
   On which your feelings
   Float?
           Aren't they also
   The banks of that stream
   And you yourself the flowing?

❧ Memories: embers.

Words stir them
And flames leap up.

We feel again

The heat of her,
The force of him.

Beloved, beloved,
Shining in the dark.

❧ Scar they stare at.
Star they're scared of.

Mark of the beloved—
A brightness that frightens.

To be touched so:
Taken past harm
To the place poems know.

PART FIVE

❦ Now the leaves are falling fiercely,
Giving themselves to the wind's
Will like a Technicolor blizzard.

Safe in my house, looking out.
Savoring the poem of wildness,
Savoring the world's unthinking
Decision to give itself over entirely.

This window between me and the world:
Like reading a page in the Book,
Taking it in deeply. Gladdened
By the swirl and swoop of it,
Gladdened by this emblem of passion.

Glad also of the glass, of the distance
That makes it safe to feel this.

❧ Not to make loss beautiful,
But to make loss the place
Where beauty starts. Where
The heart understands
For the first time
The nature of its journey.

Love, yes. The body
Of the beloved as the gift
Bestowed. But only
Temporarily. Given freely,
But now to be earned.

Given without thought,
And now loss
Has made us thoughtful.

❧ The beloved moves through the world,
  Is the world.
  Becomes the hundred things we love
  Or the one and only thing or person
  We love.
                Shifting, restless,
  Refusing to incarnate in a final form,
  As if to teach us to keep our eyes
  Moving if we want to see the bird
  Flitting from bush to tree:

  There it is! No, there. No,
  It's hidden now, you can't see it,
  But you can hear its song.

❦ The world so huge and dark
It swallows our cry.

But we're no longer lost:
The beloved has heard us
And even now approaches.

We move toward each other
Like two words
That will join in a poem.

A small poem, a little song,
But one in which we're not alone.

❧ Going to the reading,
  Hoping the poet
  Will read your poem.

  Not the one you wrote,
  But the one
  Written for you,
  That you've never heard.

🌱 You went to the reading
   Eager to hear the poet's voice,
   Believing the feeling
   Would be there as well
   As in the words themselves.

   How disappointing it was.
   Reading as if half asleep himself,
   As if she couldn't care less.

   Maybe anxious, maybe afraid
   To let the feelings show too
   Openly. But why write poems
   If not because grief or joy
   Has seized you? Why read
   Them if you don't want
   To make us weep or shout aloud?

   Think of the news you're bringing:
   The beloved is still alive!

   Message that demands singing.

❦ Expecting so much,
Needing so much,
And the poet
Delivers so little.
We turn away
In disgust.

He did his best;
She tried hard
To give form
To her love and grief.
Not their fault
That it fell flat
And we were not moved.

Maybe an old poem
You must find
In a book
On a dusty shelf.

Or one not
Written yet.

One you write yourself.

❧ Such a shaking. If the elbows
   Were held by nuts and bolts
   We'd have rattled apart.

   But sinew and socket kept
   Their grip; the body's intact.

   And to think: a poem did that.

❦ The poem didn't express
    Emotion; it *was* emotion.
    And so was I
    As I became the poem,
    As I read it aloud,
    As I rose from my daily grave.

❦ That desolation is the door:
How be surprised at that?

All those moments we shared
Only prelude to this painful
Growing. Her loss forcing
It upon us, his absence insisting.

Not bliss. Never again bliss,
But maybe a deeper knowing.

🌱 Some days it's all fuzzy.
I can't find the world,
Can't find the beloved.
Can't even find the words.

Time to lie back and listen.
Maybe something's being said,
Something I haven't heard.

Time to stop talking
And let the beloved speak.

Time to trust it all:
To stop searching
And let the beloved seek.

❧ Body of the beloved,
Body of the world.

The eyes can't cease
Their feasting.

Book of the body
Of the beloved:
Inexhaustible.

Not just the Book,
But your hunger for it.

❧ How lucky we are
That you can't sell
A poem, that it has
No value. Might
As well
Give it away.

That poem you love,
That saved your life,
Wasn't it given to you?

❧ For me, my brother
  Was the first beloved,
  The first departure
  That tore my heart.
  I was so stricken
  When he died
  I couldn't speak.

  I was young
  And knew nothing
  About the Book.

  It was years before
  I learned poems
  Could be letters
  The living address
  To their dead.
  Years before I knew
  Poems in the Book
  Were answers they send.

❦ Invisible distance between
   Yourself and the world:
   Rage layered on the body
   Like armor. Limbs
   Thick with it, stiff,
   Unable to move easily.

   Unable to touch the body
   Of the beloved because
   Inches of it cover your skin.

❧ Words not just the empty
Shells of things.
Alive, darting
Like minnows in a stream:
Flash and shimmer.

And the water itself:
The flow of our feelings –
Ripple and purl;
The tiny whirlpool
That holds the leaf
In a brief, dizzy embrace,
Then lets it go.

🌼 Hold off, rain.
   Of course, my garden
   Craves water.
   But the peonies
   Are in full blossom.
   If you fall now,
   Their petals will
   All be scattered.

   Wait a day.
   Let them feel
   The pure joy
   Of opening.

   Fall tomorrow,
   Then you can show
   Them love
   Is also a shattering.

❧ Where did the beloved go?
I've looked in all the poems,
Looked high and low.

Coming toward me,
Blank page in one hand,
Pen in the other.

Coming toward me,
A song on her lips.
Only needing me,
Only needing me for the words.

❦ Even before speech
Revealed your secret,
There was looking.

Even before song
That gave you away,
There was gazing.

The beloved felt
Your eyes upon her;
He dimly understood
Why you looked at him
That way.
          Speech
Of the eyes: the stare
And the glimpse.

The glance that lingers.

❦ The motions so cautious,
Gestures almost not worth
Making.
           Do you think
The beloved rewards this?
Have you never heard
Of extravagance?
                Love
Parceled out bit by bit
So it will last longer.

Look at the beloved –
Can't you see her laughing?

❦ To see the beloved,
   To be seen by the beloved:
   That's where being starts.

   Looking with the eyes, of course.
   But who could be filled
   With such gazing and not
   Want more?

   Looking with words also.

   Look and then leap.
   Gaze and then speak.

❧ Were we invited?
Was that what the beloved's
Smile signified?

Quick, say Yes.
Tell her we'll be there.
Tell him we can't wait.

I missed so many things
Because I was sleeping.
I don't want to miss this.

❧ Acrobatic postures I enjoyed
In my youth but
Can't even imagine now.

I could study this crude
Drawing for hours and still
Not figure out how it's done.

Some secrets and joys
Time takes downriver.
Never to be seen again.

Behind me forever:
Both the temptations of youth
And its strenuous attempts.

Settling now for the Book's
Calmer sections and pleasures.

If a peach leads you into the world,
Into an appreciation of its delights,
How much more so the beloved.

A morsel of peach meat, a single
Kiss and you know pleasure
Has depths beyond measuring.

All this not subject to loss but
Certain of it – guaranteed
To vanish. Therefore, more precious,
Therefore, brought back
By poems and songs. The mouth
Open as if to sing, as if to sink
Its brave teeth in a peach.

❦ Autumn, and the days
Grow shorter;
Squeezing the same radiance
Into a smaller space.

More intense than ever,
The beloved's lust for us.

She must know
We, too, are getting ready
To become a poem.

❧ Sudden shower
   Of golden leaves
   Descending from the maple.

   Shameless beloved,
   Undressing in public again.

❦ Do words outlast
The world
They describe?
Do the things
Fall away,
Leaving only
The husks
Of their names?

And what does
Their perishing
Ask of us?

Lift up, lift up:
A song
Could redeem them.
A poem
Could fill them
With life again.

Don't we owe
The world
At least that much,
That gave itself
So freely to us?

✿ Did the beloved die?
Yes and no.
Only really ceasing
When we cease to care.

Therefore (as Keats put it),
"On every morrow
Are we wreathing
Flowery bands
To bind us to the earth."

Which is to say:
Composing poems
And melodious songs
That celebrate the world.

Which is to say:
Helping the beloved
To be reborn
By writing and reading
Poems.

Which is to say:
We have an urgent purpose.

Which is to say.

❦ Why should it all
Be lost?
Why should time
Take away
That day by the river?

Surely, the storerooms
Of oblivion
Are full to bursting.
Surely, to bring back
That single scene
In all its glory
Wouldn't harm
The order of things.

If only in the words
Of a song or poem.
If only for a moment,
Restoring that moment.

❦ Black marks
On paper
Or parchment,
Painted
On bark.
What magic
At work here?

Are these words?
Are these
A silent saying
Of all
We hold dear?

Are these proof
Of our being,

Of our being here?

❧ No longer a part
Of the story,
Yet she's become
The story.

No longer a part
Of the world,
But he's become
The world.

Songs are forever
Saying this;
Poems knew this
From the start
Of time.
            They waited
Patiently in the Book
For that moment
When grief
Would open our ears,
When loss
Would open all of us.

You lost the beloved.
You thought: her page
Is torn from the book
Of life. You thought:
It's as if he never lived.

How wrong you were:
Loss writes so many
Poems in the Book,
Writes till its hand aches,
Till it's exhausted
And can't write anymore.

Then it sings a song.

❧ And if not you, then who?

Weren't you the one
Who cherished her,
Even from afar?

Weren't you the one
Who knew his worth,
Who knew the intensity
Of your love
Was not excessive?

How can you give up
The beloved as lost?

Always it was you:
The poems in the Book
Prove it.
          The songs
Attest to your passion.

✿ An anthology gathered
Since the beginning of time,
Gathering itself.

Only to disperse, as a tree
Scatters its leaves.
Only to tear itself apart
And give to each who needs.

❧ His song was about the world,
She sang of what she saw,
And yet it was always
The beloved's own being
That was the theme
Of that beautiful music.

Sometimes it was words,
Sometimes only the body's
Movements or an expression
Fleeting across the face.

And now the singer himself
Has fled. Now her silence
Is absolute.

Now I open the Book,
Hoping to hear that song again.

ABOUT THE AUTHOR

Gregory Orr is the author of eight previous collections of poetry, the most recent of which is *The Caged Owl: New and Selected Poems* (Copper Canyon Press, 2002). Among his other books are a memoir, *The Blessing* (Council Oak Books, 2002), which was chosen by *Publishers Weekly* as one of the fifty best nonfiction books of 2002, and *Poetry as Survival* (University of Georgia Press, 2002), a study of the cultural and psychological dynamics of the personal lyric.

He has been the recipient of a Guggenheim Fellowship and two poetry fellowships from the National Endowment for the Arts. In 2003 he was presented with the Award in Literature by the American Academy of Arts and Letters. In 2001 he was a Rockefeller Fellow at the Institute for the Study of Culture and Survival, where he began work on a study of the political and social dimension of the personal lyric.

He is a professor of English at the University of Virginia, where he has taught since 1975, and where he was the founder and first director of its MFA in Writing program. He lives with his wife, who is a painter, and his two daughters in Charlottesville, Virginia.

The Chinese character for poetry is made up of two parts: "word" and "temple." It also serves as pressmark for Copper Canyon Press. Founded in 1972, Copper Canyon Press remains dedicated to publishing poetry exclusively, from Nobel laureates to new and emerging authors. The Press thrives with the generous patronage of readers, writers, booksellers, librarians, teachers, students, and funders—everyone who shares the conviction that poetry invigorates the language and sharpens our appreciation of the world.

Major funding has been provided by:

The Paul G. Allen Family Foundation

THE **PAUL G. ALLEN FAMILY** *foundation*

Lannan Foundation

Lannan

National Endowment for the Arts

NATIONAL ENDOWMENT FOR THE ARTS

Washington State Arts Commission

WASHINGTON STATE ARTS COMMISSION

For information and catalogs:

COPPER CANYON PRESS
Post Office Box 271
Port Townsend, Washington 98368
360-385-4925
www.coppercanyonpress.org

The text is set in Dante, designed by Giovanni Mardersteig in 1954. Mardersteig was a fine printer and type designer who made his home in Verona. The titles, set in Kallos, and the ornaments were designed by British calligrapher Phill Grimshaw. Book design and composition by Valerie Brewster, Scribe Typography.